Classroom Management

in General, Choral, and Instrumental Music Programs

Classroom Management

in General, Choral, and Instrumental Music Programs

Marvelene C. Moore
with Angela L. Batey and David M. Royse

MENC MENC
MENC MENC The National Association for Music Education

Production Editor: Teresa K. Preston

Copyright © 2002
MENC—The National Association for Music Education
1806 Robert Fulton Drive, Reston, VA 20191
All rights reserved.
Printed in the United States of America.
ISBN 1-56545-149-X

Contents

Introduction

Do your students exhibit unruly behavior? Are they more interested in "acting out" than in participating in the music lesson or rehearsal? Do disruptive students dominate your classroom and infringe on the other students' right to learn? Is your class controlled by aggressive students? Do you believe your rehearsal is out of control? Are you interested in ideas which may prevent undesirable student behavior? Is your management style in need of review or fine-tuning? If you can answer yes to any of these questions, this book is for you. It is designed to provide strategies that address a variety of classroom management problems. It addresses the concerns of inexperienced music teachers, who generally rank the classroom and the rehearsal as the number one challenge in music teaching today, and it provides new ideas for those who have taught for several years.

Often, teachers find it difficult to focus on the lesson while keeping students engaged in learning. Further, they may feel the nature of music instruction produces a highly energized and electrifying classroom where students express themselves in ways that may contribute to unmanageable behavior. Challenging situations may occur in the music classroom, but there are ways to maintain appropriate student behavior.

Many educators attribute problems of student behavior in the classroom to outside factors ranging from illiteracy to relaxed standards of behavior in American society. Other factors that have been cited as sources of discipline problems are (1) the widely diverse background of students, who have individual value systems but must coexist in the classroom; (2) differences in interest, ability, and skill among students; (3) the absence of parents from the home, leaving young people to govern themselves; and (4) the increase of violence in American society.

Despite this seemingly troublesome picture, there is hope for establishing a positive classroom environment where students are actively involved in the performance and study of music while maintaining appropriate behavior. This book offers the teacher in the general, choral, and instrumental music classroom effective and innovative strategies and techniques for classroom management. It (1) describes the nature of classroom management in the areas of general, choral, and instrumental music; (2) suggests steps that can be taken to prevent behavior problems; (3) provides techniques for managing behavior; and (4) explains legal issues that pertain to classroom management. In addition, it gives suggestions for selecting repertoire that helps minimize disruptive behavior.

Defining Classroom Management

Webster's defines management as "the act or art of managing: the conducting or supervising of something" (1998). More specifically, classroom management may be defined as conducting or directing instructional activities with a degree of skill in addressing student behavior. It may also be characterized as the "orchestration of classroom life: planning curriculum, organizing procedures and resources, arranging the environment to maximize efficiency, and monitoring student progress in anticipation of potential student problems" (Lemlich, 1979, p. 5). Consequently, classroom management becomes the art of preventing behavioral problems and effectively addressing those that occur.

How a teacher employs management techniques and applies preventive measures is based on the teacher's philosophy about how students learn to conduct themselves. On the one hand, a teacher may believe that most students are unfocused and should learn to pay attention at all times. This teacher may implement a standard behavior technique for all situations. On the other hand, a teacher may believe that students should be very focused only when they are actively involved in the lesson. When behavior problems occur, this teacher may focus on the appropriate management strategy for that specific behavior (Short, Short, & Blanton, 1994, p.15).

The Center for Adolescent Studies (1996) at Indiana University has described various types of teachers and their classroom management techniques in detail. The Center identified three types of undesirable classroom management styles: authoritarian, laissez-faire, and indifferent.

The **authoritarian** teacher manages the classroom by placing strict controls on students. This type of teacher generally (1) assigns students to specific seats without allowing them to change their seating for any reason,

(2) seats students in rows where it is difficult to have eye contact with other members of the class, and (3) doesn't encourage students to move around the room for any reason. In a music classroom managed by this type of teacher, students are engaged in learning that is more academic and less skill- or performance-oriented. Improvisation and creativity are rare because the teacher fears losing control of the class. Authoritarian teachers generally do not support trips to the symphony because they believe that the same results can be accomplished in the more controlled classroom environment. Students often believe that these teachers are uncaring and aloof because they determine ideal classroom behavior without input from students or concern for their participation in the process.

The **laissez-faire** teacher allows students to do as they wish, for fear of hurting their feelings or discouraging them. This type of teacher generally (1) allows students to sit wherever they want; (2) lets students sit in rows, semicircles, on the floor, or wherever it is most comfortable for them; and (3) doesn't discourage students from moving around the room as long as they are creating, involved, and happy with their activity. In a music classroom managed by this type of teacher, creativity and improvisation may be pushed to the limits and may not be based on sound music principles. These teachers usually encourage trips to concerts and other events because they are more concerned about the students' emotional well-being and happiness than about how much music they learn. Students tend to like these teachers and regard them as friends. However, what students actually learn about music and the quality of their experiences are debatable.

The **indifferent** teacher is not interested in control or in the students' well-being. These teachers do not want to become very involved with the students and are not committed to teaching music. They often teach just to have a job and do not spend much time preparing for instruction. Usually, these teachers use the same material, in the same way, year after year, regardless of the makeup of their classes, or their students' interests and abilities. In the classroom, everyone "goes through the motions." Trips to concerts rarely happen because they are too much trouble to plan and organize. Students don't really like these teachers and can easily sense that they are not interested in the students' learning or music-making.

A more desirable management style is one that is neither authoritarian, laissez-faire, or indifferent as described by the Center for Adolescent Studies. Rather, it is the teacher who encourages independence within certain limits who is most successful in classroom management. These teachers are open to interaction with students and may allow students to interrupt with relevant questions. These teachers are **authoritative** and give careful thought to how they discipline students. Students see these teachers as fair and compassionate.

The Center has developed a questionnaire (see sidebar) to help teachers determine their management profile and decide whether they need to make changes in their classroom management techniques.

What Is Your Classroom Management Profile?

Directions: Read each statement carefully. Write your responses on a sheet of paper. Respond to each statement based upon either actual or imagined classroom experience. Then follow the scoring instructions below. Use the following scale for your responses: 1 = strongly disagree; 2 = disagree; 3 = neutral; 4 = agree; 5 = strongly agree.

(1) If a student is disruptive during class, I assign him or her to detention, without further discussion.
(2) I don't want to impose any rules on my students.
(3) The classroom must be quiet in order for students to learn.
(4) I am concerned about both what my students learn and how they learn.
(5) If a student turns in a late homework assignment, it is not my problem.
(6) I don't want to reprimand a student because it might hurt his or her feelings.
(7) Class preparation isn't worth the effort.
(8) I always try to explain the reasons behind my rules and decisions.
(9) I will not accept excuses from a student who is tardy.
(10) The emotional well-being of my students is more important than classroom control.
(11) My students understand that they can interrupt my lecture if they have a relevant question.
(12) If a student requests a hall pass, I always honor the request.

To score your quiz, add your responses to statements 1, 3, and 9. This is your score for the **authoritarian** style. Statements 4, 8, and 11 refer to the **authoritative** style. Statements 6, 10, and 12 refer to the **laissez-faire** style. Statements 2, 5, and 7 refer to the **indifferent** style.

The result of these calculations indicates your classroom management profile. Your score for each management style can range from 3 to 15. A high score indicates a strong preference for that particular style.

Note: Based on "What is your classroom management profile?" 1996, *Teacher Talk, 1* (2) [Online]. Available at http://www.education.indiana.edu/cas/. Copyright 1996 by Indiana University.

REFERENCES

Center for Adolescent Studies. (1996). What is your classroom management profile? *Teacher Talk, 1* (2) [On-line]. Available at http://www.education.indiana.edu/cas/

Lemlech, J. K. (1979). *Classroom management.* New York: Harper & Row.

Merriam-Webster's collegiate dictionary (10th ed.). (1998). Springfield, MA: Merriam-Webster.

Short, P. M., Short, R. J., & Blanton, C. (1994). *Rethinking student discipline: Alternatives that work.* Thousand Oaks, CA: Corwin Press.

Description of Behavior Management

In a music classroom, students are expected to participate in music in various ways. Activities may range from quiet listening and singing in multiple parts to playing in an instrumental ensemble. In order to manage the variety of activities in a music classroom, some teachers will insist that students follow a rigid set of rules and instructions, while others will encourage them to interact with the music and their peers. Whatever the teacher's management style, the classroom must provide an atmosphere in which all students can learn. To create this positive learning atmosphere, the music teacher must have a certain level of expertise in managing students. The teacher must know the students well, understand the subject matter, have the courage to discipline, accurately define the challenges that individual students present, and concentrate on positive solutions to problems that arise.

GENERAL MUSIC PROGRAM

Know Your Students. Students in the general music classroom range in age from 5 to 17 years. They vary in ethnicity, socioeconomic status, and degree and type of discipline administered in the home. Some students are used to a rigid form of discipline while others are not. Many students are accustomed to responding to a loud, authoritative voice while others react to a softer voice. Some students are immature socially and academically while others are well-adjusted high achievers. Regardless of the range of intellectual, social, or physical abilities, the successful general music teacher will be able to recognize these variables and devise a behavior management plan, with the help of the students, to govern everyone in the music classroom. When implementing the plan, the music teacher should also remember that all students are individuals with the right to be treated with fairness, kindness, respect, and dignity.

Knowledge Is Power. The music teacher who has begun to understand the variety of backgrounds that students bring to the classroom can use that knowledge to develop a workable classroom management plan for all students.

The first step in creating a plan is establishing guidelines. The guidelines should reflect mutual student-teacher respect, provide safety and security for teacher and students, and show a relationship to learning. Clearly stated guidelines, whether "procedure-based" (emphasis on steps for accomplishing a task) or "rule-based" (emphasis on behavior that aims at preventing undesirable conduct), will contribute to effective classroom management (Levin & Nolan, 1991). Further, the music teacher should keep in mind that modeling appropriate behavior can lead to greater success in the classroom.

Discipline Takes Courage. Establishing consequences for failure to follow rules is as important as creating those rules. Often, teachers spend more time devising rules than they spend thinking through the consequences for breaking those rules. When negative behavior occurs, the teacher who has not established consequences must invent them instead of referring to an existing plan. When this happens, the teacher risks applying different consequences for the same misbehavior. Students then see the discipline plan as unfair and may lose respect for the teacher.

The general music teacher should allow students to experience natural as well as logical consequences. Natural consequences occur without the intervention of the teacher, e.g., losing a music book because it was not stored in its proper place. Logical consequences occur through intervention by the teacher, e.g., "Mary, you dropped the note cards; please pick them up" or "John, you have the choice to stop interfering while Ben plays the drums or to change your seat." Whatever the choice of consequences, they should be explained before misbehavior occurs, be understood by the students, and be applied with consistency (Levin & Nolan, 1991).

ELEMENTARY AND MIDDLE SCHOOL CHORAL PROGRAM

Know Your Students. Students in elementary choral programs range in age from 8 to 11 years old, and in the middle school program, from ages 11 to 14. They exhibit various characteristics based on their physical, emotional, and intellectual stages of development. In general, the choral teacher can expect elementary-aged students to (1) be very active, (2) have short attention spans, (3) enjoy being in a group, (4) identify with adults as role models, (5) need to feel accepted by adults, and (6) desire praise and encouragement. Middle school students may (1) be energetic, (2) have changing moods, (3) need to be accepted by peers, (4) be very critical, (5) vary in size and height, (6) vastly differ in vocal ability, quality, and range (for example, changed and unchanged voices), and (7) have diverse musical tastes.

The degree to which students exhibit these characteristics depends on their home environment, community influences, and cultural background. Therefore, understanding the differences and similarities of these students is vital. The music teacher must be able to recognize behavior that results from the stages of development and be able to manage students in groups while addressing their individual needs. To achieve this objective, music teachers must (1) be confident, (2) recognize the potential and limitations of students, (3) like students and believe in teaching them something worthwhile, (4) be accepting of who students are, (5) have a sense of humor, and (6) believe that the process of learning is as important as the result of learning (Swears, 1984).

Knowledge Is Power. Like the general music teacher, the elementary and middle school choral teacher must establish guidelines that reflect student-teacher-peer respect and are interwoven into the learning process. The teacher should place special emphasis on behavior that prevents disruptions in the choral rehearsal. Guidelines must be clearly stated and understood by the students. Guidelines and techniques of the schoolwide management programs discussed in Chapter 6 may also apply to managing behavior in the choral classroom.

Discipline Takes Courage. In elementary and middle school choral rehearsals, students should experience the natural and logical consequences of their misbehavior. To manage these consequences, the teacher must address undesirable behavior without affecting the flow of the rehearsal. The challenge is to implement consequences with nonverbal cues and gestures whenever possible.

HIGH SCHOOL CHORAL PROGRAM
Know Your Students. The high school choir director/teacher can do absolutely everything right musically, but without a working knowledge of teenagers' ups and downs, success in teaching music will probably be

limited. Knowing students, both collectively and individually, is as important as assessing musical knowledge and abilities. Students can sense if a teacher really respects them and will usually respond with respect for the teacher—a crucial point in classroom management. Students deserve to be treated fairly with the sensitivity, care, concern, and dignity given to anyone else. When there is mutual respect in a classroom, behavior problems are likely to be drastically reduced.

Understanding and acknowledging the stages of human growth and development are critical to success in the choral classroom. High school students can go from acting like a child to acting like an adult in a matter of minutes. Teenagers are eager to be treated like adults and to be given respect and responsibilities. They can often become strong peer leaders who, by their example, can assist in classroom management. On the other hand, these students often frustrate both themselves and their teachers by slipping back into immaturity. Some are very self-conscious and react with extreme emotions that are out of proportion for the situation. Peer groups are extremely important to teenagers. Teachers can use this to their advantage by setting up leaders or officers to model good behavior.

Knowledge Is Power. The choral director/teacher who understands the forces that drive teenagers can plan music activities in such a way as to use those forces to the best advantage. By accepting students' characteristics and dealing with them creatively, the teacher can develop a classroom management style based on respect and individual responsibility. Preventive discipline, coupled with solid, enthusiastic teaching, is rooted in these very tenets.

High school students expect to have some behavior guidelines. If the teacher shows compassion and respect, students will generally accept guidelines more quickly than if the teacher is a tyrant. Students appreciate having someone who is a steady and consistently positive influence.

Discipline Takes Courage. Everyone wants to be liked. It is always nice when everyone is happy, but it rarely lasts. Teachers must realize that not everyone will like them and that there will be conflicts to resolve. At times, a teacher may hesitate to discipline a student because the discipline could damage a pleasant relationship, but the teacher must do what needs to be done in order to keep control of the classroom. Students are likely to take over if they detect fear or sense any hesitation to restore order in a chaotic classroom. If the teacher does not move quickly and decisively in such situations, students will realize that the teacher does not have the courage necessary to maintain order, and the teacher will lose the students' respect. Of course, the best situation is one where students both like and respect the teacher, but having respect is much more important than being liked. In time, students may come to like, as well as respect, the teacher.

When discipline is necessary, the teacher should disapprove of the behavior, not of the student. The music teacher should strive to approach students in a positive manner and seek to correct specific inappropriate actions. The teacher must not be goaded into issuing empty threats. Students usually recognize these threats and will continue to misbehave. The teacher must follow through on all warnings to gain and maintain the respect of students. When a teacher creates a positive and supportive classroom environment, there will most likely be fewer problems with classroom disruptions.

INSTRUMENTAL MUSIC PROGRAM

Defining the Challenge. Instrumental music programs can run from late elementary through high school, may combine both small- and large-group instruction, and often involve extracurricular ensembles. These programs require a flexible and imaginative teacher who can adapt student management strategies to fit the needs of students and schools.

First and foremost, the greatest challenge of teaching middle and high school students is—and always has been—that they are adolescents. They are not children, but they are not quite adults either. Their moods and emotions can change hourly, and their behavior can be unpredictable and irrational. Still, this is understandable when considering the impact of adolescence. It is a very difficult time for young people because of the awkwardness of their bodies, the onset of sexual maturity, the desire for peer acceptance and approval, the drive to gain personal independence and competency, the curiosity to find out about the world firsthand through experimentation, and—most significantly for teachers—their rebellious nature and desire to test limits and authority figures. However, students at this age are still seeking direction and boundaries from the adults in their lives, albeit often through a love-hate kind of relationship.

Second, as times have changed, so have the characteristics of students, and these changes influence how discipline strategies are constructed and implemented. Many more young people today come from disadvantaged, unstable, or broken homes and have greater emotional needs that must be met in school. Furthermore, with the movement for greater inclusion of special education students, especially those with emotional and/or behavioral disabilities, the needs of pupils are more varied than ever. Lastly, many areas of the country are experiencing dramatic changes in the cultural, ethnic, and religious makeup of their student bodies.

Third, changes in attitudes toward traditional forms of school discipline, corporal punishment in particular, have caused schools to develop alternative forms of discipline that are complex and may not deter the most rebellious students. School shootings and an increased awareness of sexual harassment over the past decade have brought about another shift in attitudes that has resulted in the establishment of zero-tolerance policies and more stringent student dress codes. All of this is complicated by the increasing threat of lawsuits against teachers and school districts by disgruntled parents and special interest groups.

Fourth, the nature of instrumental music creates specific kinds of discipline challenges. Enrollment in music ensembles commonly exceeds that of other academic areas. In large programs, the student-teacher ratio can be as high as one-hundred-to-one. The large number of students increases the probability of misbehavior. Because extracurricular activities and concerts are expected of school bands and orchestras, instrumental teachers must manage students for longer periods of time than other educators generally do. The opportunity for conflict increases with the amount of time students are being supervised. Finally, ensemble directors must address issues of group responsibility rather than addressing discipline only at the individual level. When pupils are tardy or absent, the entire group suffers.

Concentrating on the Positives. Despite the numerous challenges for instrumental music teachers, there are many positives working in their favor. The best, most motivated students commonly join music ensembles. Furthermore, instrumental directors usually have the same students for many years. Although the size and organization of school districts vary greatly, it is still common for teachers to be assigned students for multiple terms and often for all of middle and high school. This continuity allows for routines and expectations to be established early on and makes it easier to adapt classroom management strategies at the individual level when the only major change is student maturation. Moreover, students who will not conform to the behavioral standards of the program can be encouraged to pursue a different area where their interests will be better served. Finally, and probably most importantly, research indicates that instrumental ensemble membership is highly valued by students because they enjoy being involved in music and because music groups are important socially in their lives (Royse, 1989).

REFERENCES

Levin, J., & Nolan, J. F. (1991). *Principles of classroom management: A hierarchical approach.* Englewood Cliffs, NJ: Prentice Hall.

Royse, D. (1989). Significant predictors of concert band membership continuation or discontinuation by nonmusic major students at three selected universities (Doctoral dissertation, Kent State University, 1989). *Dissertation Abstracts International 50,* 2823.

Swears, L. (1984). *Teaching the elementary school chorus.* West Nyack, NY: Parker.

Preventive
Measures

Preventive discipline as related to classroom management is rooted in respect, individual responsibility, and positive teaching. In order to create a classroom where students can learn, unimpeded by discipline problems, the teacher must intentionally structure music activities, the rehearsal, and the physical space to encourage good behavior. While some students will have behavior problems regardless of what the teacher does, most students will cooperate when an organized, sensible discipline plan is constructed. This begins with preventive measures.

GENERAL MUSIC PROGRAM

The Best Defense Is a Good Offense. There are many techniques that general music teachers can use to prevent discipline problems in the classroom:

- Create an inviting classroom. Think of your classroom as a room in your favorite place where children live, have fun, and experience challenges and successes through music activities.
- Instruct the students in ways in which you would like to be instructed.
- Develop a positive attitude about working with students and have fun.
- Arrange chairs in half-circles or rows that allow for freedom of movement among students.
- Move around the room in close proximity to the students. Walk approximately three steps toward students who are not listening, and they will usually refocus on the music lesson. Stand between students who exhibit potential for disrupting the class.
- Reserve adequate space in the classroom for activities that require freedom of motion.

- Devise a system for distributing materials like music books and instruments. Give students specific jobs to make circulating materials and equipment easier (Cornett, 1999).
- Use a CD player with quality sound and a remote control.
- Begin the music class on time and use signals for beginning, participating in, and ending activities.
- Inspire students with your knowledge and performance of music. Show them that you are knowledgeable about other disciplines that interest them.
- Use a variety of instructional methods to promote and maintain enthusiasm for music.
- Review or memorize the procedure in your lessons to allow for appropriate interaction with students. Practice finding the CD selections with the remote or manually, and become familiar with other equipment.
- Structure music lessons that take potential management problems into account.

ELEMENTARY AND MIDDLE SCHOOL CHORAL PROGRAM

The Best Defense Is a Good Offense. Certain preventive strategies can help stop problems before they start in an elementary or middle school choir:

- Devise a plan for each choral rehearsal that allows movement among students during the rehearsal.
- Select music that is appropriate for the choral students based on their interest, ability, and maturity.
- Plan rehearsals for a hall or room with adequate space and proper lighting. The room should be as bright as possible.
- Create a seating chart with assigned seats based on student behavior, singing ability, height, and sex. Whenever possible, seat more than one girl with two or more boys.
- Enlist a student helper to check attendance.
- Prepare folders before the rehearsal and devise a system for getting and returning folders before and after the rehearsal.
- Talk less and sing more.
- Begin and end the choral rehearsal on time (Swears, 1984).

Preventive measures discussed in the general music section are also applicable to the elementary choral rehearsal.

HIGH SCHOOL CHORAL PROGRAM

The Best Defense Is a Good Offense. Planning ahead and staying organized can prevent many difficulties in the high school choir classroom.

- Be organized. Provide a clean and neat space for rehearsal. Keep chairs neatly arranged, keep trash off the floor, and fill bulletin boards with information on upcoming activities. Involve students in the caretaking process. Insist on keeping your classroom organized at all times. Even the most meager facility can show evidence of your care, and student involvement will give them a sense of ownership that will pay off in myriad ways.

- Begin the rehearsal on time. The start of class is frequently an important cog in the organizational wheel. Start your warm-up as soon as the bell stops ringing, and use the same signal to begin every day. Establish a routine for students entering the classroom. Provide a safe place where they may leave their belongings and a clear system for getting their music for rehearsal.

- Exude confidence and maintain a professional demeanor and appearance, hand-in-hand with an effective style of leadership. Reflect a sense of personal integrity and sensitivity. Your students will most likely mirror your behavior.

- Have a smooth system for taking attendance and handling music. Distributing music during class often gives students the opportunity to pull the entire class off task. Have student music librarians who hand out and take up music, and try to have music placed in each folder before rehearsal begins. Train singers to ask the student librarian for music if it is needed in the middle of rehearsal.

- Develop a set of classroom rules and be consistent. Your expectations and the consequences for breaking the stated rules should be clear.

- Treat all students with respect. Learn their names and use them in conversation. When they realize you have gone to the effort of doing that, they may begin to respect you for that alone.

- Know your music. You will then be free to move around the room, which will improve your students' behavior. By maintaining eye contact, you will encourage your singers to contribute in a positive manner and let them know you care about them and what they're doing. By the same token, having a detailed, fast-paced rehearsal plan will help keep your singers on task and less likely to be disruptive.

- Create a positive, supportive environment, not a dictatorship. Students should feel comfortable making mistakes and know they will not be embarrassed by someone they trust. Use the words "us" and "we."
- Minimize your off-topic talk during rehearsal. When you "get down to business," students are likely to do the same. Give concise instructions. Place general announcements about halfway through the rehearsal or after working on a piece that requires a lot of vocal work. This gives the voice a chance to rest. Never get into a situation when you must ask each class member for information, (i.e., phone numbers). Keep everyone on task by working with the entire group as much as possible.
- Monitor your students' body language and demeanor to prevent fatigue and frustration. Students who are frustrated and tired are more likely to misbehave. If the level of talking in the classroom is keeping learning from taking place and you are unable to maintain discipline, stop and remain still and silent until the students realize you have stopped. Never get into a shouting match. The students will win.
- Place students in roles of leadership. Often, a system of this type will provide you with positive role models and can be so effective that you will have no need to discipline students. The use of a formal choir council to hold students accountable for their behavior can be more effective than a thousand phone calls home!

INSTRUMENTAL MUSIC PROGRAM

An Ounce of Prevention Is Worth a Pound of Cure. There are several things band and orchestra teachers can do to avoid problem behavior. To begin with, make sure students know exactly what is expected of them and what the consequences are for not conforming to the conduct standards of the group. Establish clear, enforceable rules and procedures at the beginning of the school year. Integrate those rules into a workable system and teach it to students. While this seems sensible, some ensemble directors feel uneasy about starting off the year with a declaration of rules because they fear it will create a negative tone or take too much time away from rehearsal. However, research indicates that this is a method utilized by effective classroom managers and a wise investment of time (Doyle, 1986). In the long run, this approach is likely to pay off.

Give Them a Meal, Not a Snack. Actively engage students in quality learning experiences. This is likely to increase student achievement and diminish problem behavior (Duke, 1999/2000). Plan numerous music-making opportunities with an uncompromising standard of excellence. Through creative concert programming using quality literature, give performers something meaningful to work toward. Supplement large-ensemble performances with small-group and individual opportunities, private lessons, and honors ensembles. Through such a balanced program, students will experience success and recognition from peers and family and find that ensemble membership is worthy of their time and energies.

Structure the Rehearsal with Discipline in Mind. With the right rehearsal structure, you can prevent many off-task behaviors (Doyle, 1986). Establish a regular routine so performers know what is expected. This minimizes discussion and allows the rehearsal to begin immediately and flow throughout the period. Start on time and make sure the rehearsal goes to the end of the period, leaving only enough time for instruments to be put away. Unruly behavior commonly occurs during the transitional times at the beginning and end of rehearsal.

Plan the most detailed work immediately after warm-up because students are most attentive early in the period. Usually the younger the group, the more this is true. Keep the pace moving along, rehearsing more at the ensemble level as the period progresses. This keeps more students engaged and provides fewer opportunities for discipline problems as the group tires. Selections should not be practiced over and over simply to avoid behavioral problems, but some aspects of perfecting a musical selection do need to be done at the ensemble level. Examples of this include working on ensemble balance, blend, tempo, and stylistic interpretation. The latter part of the rehearsal is also a good time to play through previously prepared works to keep them fresh with the group. It is also an appropriate time for sight-reading, which by its nature keeps everyone on task. Schedule sectionals. There are fewer discipline problems with a smaller group, and it is possible to get more done.

Win Them Over to Your Side. Gain students' trust and respect by displaying a genuine, caring attitude toward them and their interests. Go out of your way to give students every opportunity to succeed and don't give up on those who fall short. Treat students equally and fairly and, when disciplining, make a point to separate the person's action from the person. Over time, these humane qualities will lead your ensemble members to feel a great deal of respect, and often fondness, for you. Be that as it may, some teenagers may not readily show this, as they are often loath to demonstrate such things publicly. Usually, however, parents will know if you are making a difference in their child's life, and they will be a supporting influence in the home. In the long run, this will make a difference in the classroom and sometimes win over even the most difficult students.

Nurture Peer Discipline. When students take pride in their ensemble, they will work toward its betterment and even monitor each other's behavior. Mature pupils understand that their behavior directly impacts the quality of the ensemble's performance and that it is better to work with directors rather than against them. This starts with the upperclassmen and section leaders, who should be expected to both model appropriate behavior for the group and monitor the behavior of underclassmen. Help your student leaders develop their leadership skills and prepare them to handle minor errant behaviors. Be sure to handle major discipline decisions yourself in order to fulfill the legal expectations of due process.

Publish a Handbook. Document the rules and procedures in a written handbook and share it with students, parents, and administrators. The basic framework for the document should come from approved policies of the school system and be customized to fit the needs of the instrumental program. Include grading practices, attendance policies, and organizational issues, such as election of officers or yearly awards. Involve students in the preparation of the document to assure ownership and a greater understanding of the need for such rules. Once the handbook is in the final-draft form, ask the school's administration to approve it before distributing it to students and parents.

Prepare an Activities Calendar. By taking the time to carefully plan the semester's activities (the entire year's when possible), you can avoid most serious scheduling conflicts or at least know about them in advance so that accommodations can be made. The calendar may be organized by the month and include out-of-school rehearsals, performances, booster group meetings, awards banquets, and anything else that would be important for parents and students to know. Include the dates for the SAT or ACT, as many high school students take one or both of these tests numerous times. Post the calendar in the classroom, distribute it to students on the first day of the semester, and send a copy home to parents. Share copies with the school's administration and teachers, especially those who sponsor school activities in which ensemble students participate.

Utilize Technology for Communication. A Web site is a very efficient, up-to-date vehicle for promoting and presenting the instrumental program to the public. Besides including the basic facts about the program, it is a good place to post rules, procedures, and the activities calendar. Be sensitive to the privacy rights of students and avoid posting personal information there.

Compile e-mail lists with both parents' and students' addresses and send them news and reminder notices. This is inexpensive, immediate, and efficient. Some may argue that students should be responsible and remember things on their own, but a few friendly reminders can be helpful, especially for busy parents. As both the Web site and e-mail lists will take much time and energy in order to make them run professionally, you could delegate these duties to a booster parent or responsible student.

REFERENCES

Cornett, C. E. (1999). *The arts as meaning makers.* Upper Saddle River, NJ: Prentice Hall.

Doyle, W. (1986). Classroom organization and management. In M. C. Wittrock (Ed.), *Handbook of research on teaching* (3rd ed., pp. 392–431). New York: Macmillan.

Duke, R. (Winter 1999/2000). Measures of instructional effectiveness in music research. *Bulletin of the Council for Research in Music Education,* No. 143, 1–48.

Swears, L. (1984). *Teaching the elementary school chorus.* West Nyack, NY: Parker.

Management Strategies and Techniques

Music is a magical and powerful art. Its wonderful power can be felt deeply by the performer and the audience alike. It is the primary responsibility of the teacher to bring this powerful medium to students in the general, choral, and instrumental classroom. For the teacher to accomplish this goal, student behavior must remain within acceptable guidelines.

The goal of management, however, is not simply to keep students quiet and passive, as this does not ensure that learning is taking place. Sometimes students are not discipline problems but they are also not learning anything. A combination of good classroom management strategies and techniques, quality learning experiences, and active involvement by students is needed to ensure successful music learning, performance, and appreciation. This all begins with the teacher.

GENERAL MUSIC PROGRAM

Management strategies for the general music classroom should vary in intensity depending on the misbehavior of the students. Some behaviors require minor intervention while others demand moderate to extensive interventions.

Intervention Strategies. Minor interventions are applied to situations where little time is given to the misbehavior and instruction is not completely disrupted. Minor interventions include (1) nonverbal cues, such as making eye contact or a hand-on-head signal, (2) keeping the activity moving by making effective transitions between activities, (3) circulating in close proximity to the student, (4) issuing a brief desist by simply saying "stop," or (5) using the "I" message, which involves stating the problem, describing the effect, and explaining how the situation makes you, the teacher, feel (Emmer, Evertson, & Worsham, 2000).

Moderate interventions are more confrontational and may be more contentious. They include (1) withholding a privilege, (2) isolating or removing students, (3) using a fine or penalty, (4) assigning detention, or (5) using a consequence from the school-based system (Emmer, Evertson, & Worsham, 2000).

Extensive interventions are implemented when students continue to disrupt the class and prevent their own learning and that of others. They may include (1) designing a contract with the individual student, (2) holding a conference with parents, (3) using a check or demerit system, or (4) using a five-step intervention procedure (see table 1). By using a five-step intervention plan, you can demonstrate to students, parents, and administrators that you have given misbehaving students ample opportunities to correct their behavior.

Table 1. FIVE-STEP INTERVENTION PLAN

Step	Procedure	Example
1	Non-verbal cue	Raised index finger
2	Verbal cue	"Steve, please follow our classroom rules and our plans for creating an enjoyable music classroom."
3	Indicate choice student is making.	"Steve, if you continue to talk while I am talking, you will be choosing to go to the back of the room to develop a plan."
4	Student moves to a designated area to develop a plan for behaving appropriately.	"Steve, you have chosen to go to the back of the room to develop a plan."
5	Student is required to go somewhere else to develop a plan for behaving appropriately.	"Steve, because you are choosing not to be responsible, you will have to see Mrs. Johnson to develop your plan."

Note. From *Classroom Management for Secondary Teachers* (p.181), by E. Emmer, C. Evertson, and M. Worsham, 2000, Boston, MA: Allyn & Bacon. Copyright 2000 by Allyn & Bacon. Reprinted/adapted with permission.

Facilitating Music Skills. In addition to intervention, you can implement other teaching strategies that may be effective in reducing misbehavior. As you prepare lessons that focus on skill development, you may find these strategies helpful in teaching the following skills:

- *Singing.* Select literature that is appropriate for students' physical, intellectual, and emotional growth and development. Include contemporary songs and instrumental music literature that many students enjoy, including blues, jazz, gospel, and country music.
- *Listening.* Be familiar with the music and provide information on the composer, performer, and specific components of the music. Also make connections with other disciplines.
- *Moving.* Prepare students for movement activities and dance by instructing them in preparatory experiences in previous lessons.
- *Reading.* Allow students to chant rhythmic notation to contemporary music and sight-read pitches to contemporary music using solfège.
- *Playing Instruments.* Assist students in sharing instruments by devising an orderly system of passing them to each other without your help.
- *Creating.* Provide students with a germ of an idea from which they can construct their own compositions.

Cooperative Learning Strategies. Generally, students will advance more rapidly in the development of musical skills when they have the opportunity to work with each other. In *Schools without Failure,* William Glaser (1968) stated that students learn and retain 10% of what they hear, 80% of what they experience, and 95% of what they teach each other. If Glaser's findings are true, students acquire greater knowledge and retain more experiences when interacting with each other. It behooves the music teacher, then, to help students work together to solve problems and experience music.

Cooperative learning strategies provide those opportunities and reinforce the importance of students taking responsibility for their own learning. The strategies work well in facilitating learning among groups comprised of two to six students. The optimal size of the group is usually determined by the complexity of the assignment; small groups are best for simple problems and larger groups work well for more complex tasks. The makeup of the groups should be heterogeneous to allow for greater diversity in solving problems.

Cooperative learning strategies may be classified in three categories: (1) partners, (2) groups of four, and (3) groups of four or more (Kaplan & Stauffer, 1994). See the sidebar for a sampling of strategies in each of these three categories.

A Sampling of Cooperative Learning Strategies

PARTNERS

Think-Pair-Share. Students think to themselves about a question posed by the teacher. After a specified time, they pair up to discuss and compare their individual ideas; then the pairs share their thoughts with the whole class.

Inside-Outside-Circle. This is a variation on Think-Pair-Share, calling for two concentric circles with students facing partners. The teacher asks a question, and the partners work together to arrive at an answer. Then students in the outer circle move one place to the right to a new partner and prepare for the next question.

GROUPS OF FOUR

Three-Step Interview. Students pair up, the teacher asks a question, and the pairs go through the following three steps:

(1) After a specified time to think about the question, one student in each pair interviews the other.
(2) Partners reverse roles.
(3) Each student introduces the individual he or she interviewed to another pair and tells what was learned from the interview.

Pairs Check. This technique works best in teams of two pairs each. Students work in pairs to solve a series of problems, with one "solving" and one "coaching" for each problem and then reversing roles for the next problem. After every two problems, the pair checks with the other pair in the team to determine whether they have the same answers.

GROUPS OF FOUR OR MORE

Roundtable. The teacher asks a question. One piece of paper and a pencil are passed from student to student. Each student writes one answer or comment and then passes the paper on to the next student. A group list of answers is generated for discussion.

Jigsaw. Each student in a cooperative group is assigned only one piece of information that the group needs in order to answer a larger question or complete an assignment. They "jigsaw" out of their cooperative group and form "expert" groups made up of other class members who have been assigned the same question for their cooperative groups. Students work together in the "expert" groups, and then "jigsaw" back to their original cooperative groups to teach what they have learned. The focus is on sharing information with others.

Note. Based on information from *Cooperative Learning in Music* by P. R. Kaplan and S. L. Stauffer 1994, Reston, VA: MENC.

Cooperative learning strategies provide opportunities for students to discover the many ways in which they are alike and different. Through their interaction, students acquire respect for themselves and others. Students learn to have regard for the opinions, ideas, and musical performances of classmates. They begin to acquire the ability to (1) listen without interrupting, (2) think critically and present opposing opinions in appropriate ways, (3) receive criticism from others, (4) stay on task, (5) encourage and support their peers, (6) ask questions appropriately by raising their hands and speaking at an acceptable volume, (7) monitor the use of their time, and (8) express their feelings in ways that are not disruptive, violent, or otherwise socially unacceptable.

ELEMENTARY AND MIDDLE SCHOOL CHORAL PROGRAM

The elementary and middle school chorus are places where students can learn the importance of proper group behavior while acquiring skills for functioning independently and acting responsibly. In order to foster these qualities in students, it is important to carefully plan strategies that facilitate this development.

- Share and display guidelines early in the academic year. On the first day of the rehearsal, tell students how they are expected to behave. Display a written description of the expectations at a prominent place in the room to serve as a reminder. Guidelines may include these statements: (1) enter and leave the rehearsal room quietly, (2) talking is permitted before and after the rehearsal only, (3) always remember your folder, and (4) raise your hand when you have a question (Swears, 1984).
- Establish a routine for the rehearsal. Students in elementary and middle school like consistency because it gives them greater security. A routine provides stability and helps establish expectations. Consequently, you should repeat certain portions of the rehearsal on a regular basis.
- Carefully choose ways to discipline. Because of the nature of choral singing, stopping to address discipline problems impedes the flow of the rehearsal. Create hand signals and gestures to manage inappropriate behavior during the rehearsal and talk with students one-on-one at the end of the class. Stop the rehearsal and take care of the behavior problems only when it becomes necessary.
- Plan for a lively rehearsal. Keep the rehearsal moving. Proceed quickly from one activity to the next. Avoid lag time between songs, exercises, and announcements.

- Talk little; sing more. Students can easily become bored if you give too much information prior to beginning the rehearsal and between the songs; use an economy of words so that students can maintain focus.
- Secure student helpers. Elementary and middle school students are eager to help their teacher. They are willing to arrange chairs, organize music in folders, take attendance, decorate bulletin boards, file papers, and so on. Ask students to perform these tasks, so you can devote more time to the music and other aspects of the rehearsal. This kind of involvement creates a greater sense of belonging among students (Swears, 1984).

HIGH SCHOOL CHORAL PROGRAM

The Curriculum. The music selected to be rehearsed and performed is the very heart of the choral curriculum. Choices in this realm are likely to affect everything else that transpires during the year. Make your decisions with a great deal of thought and consideration because the music you choose speaks volumes to students and parents about you as a musician and music educator. Selecting music that challenges your singers, planning and pacing your rehearsal carefully, and showing students that you care enough about them to ask them to do their very best will set the tone for what happens each and every day in the classroom.

As a result of studying the chosen pieces, students should become improved singers and more intelligent musicians. To achieve this end, choose several selections that stretch their abilities, but be sure to include pieces that resonate with them as well. A good balance for any choir is for the majority of music to be just at or slightly above singers' current level of musical ability, for several pieces to be difficult, and for several others to be pieces that can quickly be brought to performance-ready status. Integrate the teaching of sight-singing skills, vocal technique, style, history, aural skills, basic theory, and music terminology into each day's rehearsal. If you include these aspects of music, rehearsal pacing should be at such a level as to prevent many potential discipline problems.

Plan to Succeed. More often than not, a poorly planned rehearsal will deteriorate rapidly. Studying the score in advance and carefully planning the rehearsal will allow freedom to monitor the atmosphere and movements in your classroom. If your nose is not in the score, your focus is exactly where it needs to be—on your students and their interaction with you, the music, and each other. If students know that you have spent valuable time getting prepared and organized for their rehearsal, they will

Classroom Management

know that their efforts are important. Score study as a tool for management cannot be overemphasized. The evidence of your ation as a teacher starts here.

The First Day. Begin your first class of the year with a medium-to-difficult piece from the previous year, preferably in a foreign language, and move your rehearsal very quickly. This reminds your returning members of the level of discipline and commitment expected, it shows the new members what is expected of them, and it keeps students from filling out yet another information sheet for yet another teacher—a welcome relief. It also shows students that you are committed to the subject matter and are not using the first day as an excuse not to teach. Quickly define for the students what you consider a positive attitude: paying attention, having all music and a pencil, being on time, following directions, not talking during rehearsal, using good posture, and other characteristics that you deem important. To establish a disciplined classroom, you will have to rehearse consistently from bell to bell on a daily basis. This means no free days—not even as a reward for good behavior.

How to Start. When your students come to class, they bring with them all the emotional baggage of their previous school day. It is up to you to focus their energy and thoughts on the music. Use warm-up exercises to accomplish this. Conventional wisdom tells us that using the same warm-ups every day invites our singers to complacency. Though this may be true, you can still be very successful by starting each warm-up session with a single pitch on a neutral syllable just as soon as the bell stops ringing. Have students hold this pitch for about ten seconds to allow everyone to settle in; then modify it to all vowels. This is both an attention-getting device and a signal that rehearsal has started. If you begin with this simple exercise every day, most students will quickly get the idea that you are serious about beginning your rehearsal on time and working with them to achieve quality results. After this initial exercise, vary the warm-ups from day to day to keep students involved and to focus their minds on the task at hand.

The First Piece. Choose the first piece with care as it will establish the tone of the entire rehearsal. Generally speaking, moderate to moderately fast pieces work well in this position. Consider using a piece with limited ranges to help in warming up the voice. Reviewing an area of a selection that was successful in the preceding rehearsal is also a great technique to get the singers to quickly concentrate and focus.

the Middle. Rehearse the music in need of the most work in the middle of the class period. Singers will be more likely to keep their energy and attention for longer periods of time during the early to middle rehearsal and after tasting success with the first piece. Always be sensitive to your singers' fatigue or frustration levels. Twenty minutes on one piece is close to the saturation point for high school students. Watch for and heed signals of restlessness or boredom during rehearsal and modify your plans accordingly. Your face should show the mood of each piece and how you feel about the music, the singers, and their efforts. Pay attention to your rehearsal demeanor because students will mirror what you do. The same holds true with talking. If you talk too much during rehearsal, your students will too.

Pacing is an important key to maintaining discipline. When stopping to give instructions and asking the choir to begin again, do not allow too much time for everyone to find the place. Instead, train students to hear instructions for starting the first time. To keep everyone on task, maintain student involvement with the rehearsal. The possibilities are endless here: Ask everyone to sing one part. Ask some voice parts to hum while the others sing text. Alternate. Ask some voice parts to count-sing while others sing text. Keep the rehearsal moving, but be sure to allow for student interaction within the context of a managed classroom. Do not make the mistake of being all work and no play. Students will appreciate your willingness to laugh at yourself and admit mistakes you make. It makes you more human.

Leave Them Wanting More. Vary the styles of pieces as the rehearsal progresses. Be careful not to rehearse two similar pieces back to back. Try to rehearse a piece that students like after one on which they have worked hard. Send them out of your classroom smiling. Make sure that they leave your rehearsal with a "good taste" in their mouths by singing something that will not only provide closure for that rehearsal but will also create anticipation and excitement about the next one.

The final thing your students should hear from you each day is how much you have appreciated their efforts. They need your positive feedback and will most likely work harder and be more disciplined if they know that what they are doing is appreciated. This step firmly establishes a positive atmosphere from day to day and will generally pay great dividends in classroom management. If your students know that you truly care about their success and respect them as individuals, there will most likely be success in the classroom. Even if the rehearsal was not especially productive, give stu-

Classroom Management

dents a positive evaluation as to why they were unsuccessful in that rehearsal. Be sure to give them a reason to want to come back to your classroom.

INSTRUMENTAL MUSIC PROGRAM

Establish Your Comfort Zone. The first step in establishing effective rehearsal room management is coming to grips with your comfort zone for student behavior, also referred to as teacher style. Although some people have absolutist views about student conduct, the truth is that music teachers with excellent instrumental programs vary greatly in their attitudes toward student behavior. Some are very strict disciplinarians while others feel comfortable with a more relaxed style of management. The most important consideration is that behavior is appropriate enough so that all students have an opportunity to learn in a safe environment. Consequently, certain actions should never be tolerated. These include overt disrespect for the teacher, threatening or striking fellow students, destruction of school property, swearing or foul language, and using alcohol or drugs on school grounds.

Practice Enthusiasm. Research has indicated a relationship between enthusiasm and timing of effective activities with effective classroom management (Madsen, Standley, & Cassidy, 1989). This would suggest that it is worthwhile to be enthusiastic. For some people, enthusiasm comes naturally and spontaneously; however, for people with a more staid personality, enthusiasm is harder to produce. Still, anyone can generate some enthusiasm in their professional lives, especially music teachers, who are performers to begin with. Anyone can walk fast, talk quickly, and get excited about little things in life. It begins with looking for the good in each situation and letting the world know about it. Interestingly, over time it is difficult to tell if some teachers are enthusiastic because they believe they should be or because they really are. It really doesn't matter as long as enthusiasm is present.

Be Demanding. Over the years, research has consistently indicated that effective instrumental music teachers hold high expectations for their pupils (Saunders & Worthington, 1990). This is true not only academically, but behaviorally as well. From the first contact with students, insist on adherence to the rules and ensure that student behavior is appropriate for the situation at hand. Many teachers are constantly frustrated by recurring student problems that are often of their own making. The students are unruly simply because the teacher allows them to be. This often happens with young educators who want to be liked. This usually comes back to haunt them later on, however, as they realize the need for greater classroom control. Regrettably, by then they have most likely undermined their authority. Experienced ensemble directors know that being demanding shows you care and that students will come to realize that over time.

Hold Students Accountable. For the average middle and high school student, unruly behavior is rarely the result of ignorance. From the moment students enter the schoolhouse door, they are taught the rules and routines of the school. They quickly learn what conduct is appropriate and what the consequences are for disruptive actions. For the most part, student-teacher conflicts over behavior occur when students choose to ignore what they have been taught. The reasons for this vary by child and situation, but the causes of such misbehavior commonly include insecurity, impulsiveness, rebellion, peer pressure, or envy—to name only a few. Ideally, students should demonstrate the self-discipline necessary for supporting an orderly, safe learning environment for all. Because of the immaturity of children and adolescents, it is up to the teacher to hold students accountable for their actions and continually reinforce the value of personal responsibility. Simply expecting appropriate behaviors because those are the "teacher's rules" can work in the short term but may not always be in the students' best interest over time, especially for those at-risk students who are not taught these values at home.

Integrate the Curriculum with Discipline Strategies. A common misconception about teaching instrumental music is that it is a two-part process. Part one is the director instructing students. Part two is the director managing the classroom. These two activities, curriculum and management, are really inseparable. Everything done and taught in the classroom influences student behavior (Brigham, Renfro, & Brigham, 1997). To be effective, you must think through the process of instruction and decide what is to be taught and which teaching techniques will best promote good behavior. For example, when teaching phrasing, ask yourself if it would be better to give a ten-point lecture about how to produce a good phrase or to have the ensemble practice good phrasing techniques during warm-up. When teaching double tonguing to trumpets, ask yourself if it would be better to introduce this technique during a full-ensemble rehearsal or to present it during a sectional. When teaching the B-minor scale, consider whether it would be best to have the students use their notebooks to practice writing it or for you to distribute a prepared worksheet. These are only a few questions that

Classroom Management

you need to consider when planning for instruction. Many approaches can produce positive results, but depending on your management style and the students being taught, some ways may be better than others.

Have Eyes in the Back of Your Head. Before you can address off-task behavior, you must know when it is occurring. To begin with, this means identifying any behavior that is not immediately related to the class lesson. This ranges from nondisruptive daydreaming to more disorderly actions, such as talking out of turn or throwing items. (Although teachers are concerned primarily with unruly behavior, passive off-task behaviors also impact student achievement.) In other words, you must know what is going on in every inch of the rehearsal room every second of the period. This requires keen observation skills and constant monitoring of students, including their body language. This process begins with your eyes. If they are buried in the score or staring at the floor in thought, then the students have leeway to go off-task or engage in sophomoric behavior. This also calls for attentive listening. Sometimes the noises students make can be a little too cheerful, a little too aggressive, or even sometimes a little too quiet. This could signal that something is up and a class disruption is brewing.

Teach More; Talk Less. Many music teachers are born with the gift of gab. This can be a mixed blessing when working with adolescents. On one hand, students can learn a good deal from a speech that you deliver on a topic such as group dynamics and individual responsibility. However, this tool is only effective when used sparingly, such as in response to a particularly troublesome incident. The same is not as true when it comes to teacher talk during daily rehearsals. If feedback or directions are too lengthy or redundant, students will quickly lose focus and drift off task. Make points quickly and concisely, and get the students immediately back to the task at hand. This keeps things moving along smoothly and the students actively engaged.

Adjust to the Size of the Group. Common sense would suggest that music teachers have fewer discipline problems with small groups of students than with large groups. Accordingly, rehearsal techniques and management strategies must be adapted to fit the ensemble size. In general, a good rule of thumb is: the larger the group, the more teacher-directed the instruction should be. What this means practically is that you should minimize interruptions when working with very large numbers. You can do this by appointing responsible students to handle such interruptions as phone calls or visitors at the door and by taking non-immediate questions from students at a time when discipline is less of a concern, such as before and after rehearsal. Limit large-group instructional time to short, relevant comments about musical concepts, and get the group back to performing.

Stop the Problem before it Snowballs. Another area of concern when working with an ensemble is the accumulating effect of individual conduct on that of the group. Once a student starts a minor off-task behavior, other students can pick it up until it rapidly grows into disruption. This is especially true with younger students, who normally have shorter attention spans and quicker emotional shifts. This is even true with the better students, who are often fun-loving extroverts eager for attention. Still, for all age levels, it is generally true that unrest is more likely to spread quickly in large groups. As a result, you must be acutely aware of the most minute rumblings of unrest. Once detected, intervene immediately before rowdy behavior escalates. If you wait too long before addressing the problem, then it becomes more difficult to bring the group back to task. You may also be forced to give more reprimands to more people than if the problem had been handled sooner.

Avoid Needless Questions. All education majors are told that asking questions is a good thing to do. As a teaching technique, it helps with student motivation, engagement, and assessment. Even so, not every question is a good question. In fact, some can even hinder ensemble discipline. "Are you ready?" is an example of a needless question, as it is your responsibility to assess the group and decide when to start. Asking this question invites an unnecessary response that could break the flow of rehearsal. Even worse, it can build the expectation within the ensemble that the students control the downbeat. Another needless statement is, "Raise your hand if you don't understand." Students who truly don't understand will rarely admit it and risk embarrassment. Again, it is up to you to evaluate student understanding and respond accordingly. Finally, sometimes it is better to avoid asking questions at all. This is particularly true when working with large groups, such as a room full of antsy sixth-grade beginners. By the time you ask a question, choose a volunteer, and get an answer, some beginners could have their instruments disassembled. If you add follow-up questions, then total chaos can quickly develop. It is better to be task-oriented and keep things moving.

Develop a Response Plan. Regardless of how carefully you prepare and administer classroom management strategies, unruly behavior will occur. That is simply part of working with young people. Therefore, it is important to have a response plan in place to address unruly behavior. Any such plan must begin with the approved policies of the school; some schools even require that a prescribed discipline method be followed. Generally speaking, when dealing with minor infractions by individual students, it is common to discuss the situation first with the student, preferably in private. If the errant behavior continues, then the next logical step is to confer with a parent or guardian. If the problem continues, then the school's administration often becomes involved. Along the way, you may administer consequences consistent with school policy. Fit the severity of the punishment with the behavior being addressed.

REFERENCES

Brigham, F., Renfro, A., & Brigham, M. (1997). Linking music curriculum to teacher and student behavior. *Update: Application of Research in Music Education, 15* (2), 24–28.

Emmer, E. T., Evertson, C. M., & Worsham, M. E. (2000). *Classroom management for secondary teachers.* Boston: Allyn & Bacon.

Glaser, W. (1968). *Schools without failure.* New York: Harper & Row.

Kaplan, P., & Stauffer, S. (1994). *Cooperative learning in music.* Reston, VA: MENC.

Madsen, C., Standley, J., & Cassidy, J. (1989). Demonstration and recognition of high and low contrasts in teacher intensity. *Journal of Research in Music Education, 37* (2), 85–92.

Saunders, T. C., & Worthington, J. (1990). Teacher effectiveness in the performance classroom. *Update: Application of Research in Music Education, 8* (2), 26–29.

Swears, L. (1984). *Teaching the elementary school chorus.* West Nyack, NY: Parker.

Schoolwide Behavior Management Systems

Approaches to classroom management are as varied as the teachers who implement them. However, some systems for managing behavior may be adopted by an entire school or community and be implemented in all of the classrooms within the school, thus unifying the student body in a common acceptable behavior. Character Counts and Skill Streaming are two management systems that fall within this category. These systems have proven to be very successful when used by general, choral, and instrumental music teachers.

CHARACTER COUNTS

Character Counts was developed at the Josephson Institute of Ethics in Marina Del Ray, California. The concept was developed in 1992 when a group of educators, ethicists, and nonprofit leaders met in Aspen, Colorado, to discuss a Josephson Institute study in which approximately 9,000 high school and college students revealed that lying, cheating, and stealing were routine. The group thought this trend was alarming and decided to form an action group called the Character Counts Coalition to address the issue. As a result of their initiatives, the coalition was able to acquire congressional support from a group of U.S. Senators.

The resulting Character Counts program attempts to instill specific ethical values, called "Pillars of Character," in students. The pillars are trustworthiness, respect, responsibility, fairness, caring, and citizenship. All students are expected to adhere to the pillars regardless of race, gender, politics, or creed.

The Coalition promotes the belief that the six pillars are "worthy of promotion where they are evident and worthy of repair where they have faltered." The Coalition's Web site (www.charactercounts.org) documents how the six pillars were effectively emphasized at several locations, including an elementary school in Albuquerque, New Mexico. Students were asked to focus on specific behaviors (related to one of the six pillars) that emphasize a positive character trait each week, for a total of six weeks. Posters providing information about the pillar selected for the week were placed around the school to remind the students of the behavior expected of them. The posters gave descriptions of appropriate and inappropriate behavior for each pillar. The six pillars and their behaviors are the following:

- *Trustworthiness.* Be honest. Don't lie, cheat, or steal. Be reliable. Do what you say you'll do. Have the courage to do the right thing. Build a good reputation. Be loyal. Stand by your family, friends, and country.
- *Respect.* Treat others with respect. Follow the Golden Rule. Be tolerant of differences. Use good manners, not bad language. Be considerate of the feelings of others. Don't threaten, hit, or hurt anyone. Deal peacefully with anger, insults, and disagreements.
- *Responsibility.* Do what you are supposed to do. Persevere and keep on trying. Always do your best. Use self-control. Be self-disciplined. Think before you act; consider the consequences. Be accountable for your choices.
- *Fairness.* Play by the rules. Take turns and share. Be open-minded and listen to others. Don't take advantage of others. Don't carelessly blame others.
- *Caring.* Be kind. Be compassionate and show you care. Express gratitude. Forgive others. Help people in need.
- *Citizenship.* Do your share to make your school and community better. Cooperate. Stay informed and vote. Be a good neighbor. Obey laws and rules. Respect authority. Protect the environment (Josephson Institute of Ethics, 2001).

The success of Character Counts in the classroom can be found in the reports of several schools on the benefits of implementing the system. Numerous stories can be found at the Character Counts Web site (www.charactercounts.org).

If you use Character Counts in a music classroom, when respect is the pillar for the week, ask students who disrupt the class during a listening lesson if they are (1) showing respect for the music, (2) exhibiting consideration for their peers' right to listen, (3) demonstrating regard for their peers' interest in learning, (4) showing respect for the teachers, or (5) taking responsibility for their actions. When you ask questions of this nature, students are forced to stop and think about their actions and are given an opportunity to improve on their behavior.

SKILL STREAMING

While Character Counts is effective in dealing with traditional types of student behavior in the general and music education classroom, Skill Streaming offers suggestions for controlling severe behavior as well.

Skill Streaming is a school management system that focuses attention on aggressive, reclusive, and immature student behavior. It highlights the necessity of teaching students to prevent conflict or to react to conflict in a socially acceptable manner. It answers questions that teachers frequently ask about student behavior: "Why do so many of my students show disrespect to their fellow students and to their teachers?" "When students misbehave they know what the consequences will be, so why don't they change?" "I have a student in my class who is ostracized by everyone and I can certainly understand why, but what can I do for a child like that?" (McGinnis & Goldstein, 1984). Skill Streaming offers a resolution to these behavior problems through the application of psycho-educational techniques that are an integral part of the structured learning method.

The techniques found in structured learning consist of four behavioral approaches that music teachers can use. They are modeling, role-playing, performance feedback, and transfer of training. When these techniques are applied, students (1) observe teachers engaging in the acceptable behavior (modeling), (2) portray the behavior observed (role-playing), (3) discuss and receive feedback from their peers on their portrayal of the behavior (performance feedback), and (4) perform the accepted modeled behavior in another classroom situation and in the home and the community (transfer of training).

Modeling is usually successful with students in all grades. It is based on three types of imitation, (1) observational learning that incorporates new behavior previously unknown by the student, (2) inhibitory and disinhibitory effects that reinforce positive behavior and punish undesirable behavior, and (3) behavioral facilitation that embraces positive behavior known by the student. Modeling works best when students are asked to imitate individuals or teachers whom they like and with whom they share a similar background and when students receive a reward for imitating the behavior (McGinnis & Goldstein, 1984).

Role-playing involves students performing a characterization other than their own. It gives them the opportunity to play a different role, be committed to the role, improvise with the role, and be rewarded for playing the role (Mann, 1956).

Performance feedback is the act of providing input on student role-playing. Other students who observe the role-playing may offer suggestions for improvement and/or provide social reinforcement or a tangible reward (McGinnis & Goldstein, 1984).

Transfer of training refers to how well students perform acceptable behavior skills in settings other than the classroom, such as at home, on the streets, in the neighborhood, at community centers, and so on. Transfer may or may not be successful depending on the teaching setting, personnel and materials, reinforcement system, and the type of behavior instruction employed (McGinnis & Goldstein, 1984).

In the music classroom, you can use psycho-educational techniques to teach acceptable behavior. For example, when playing listening examples for students, you may *model* appropriate behavior by (1) demonstrating interest and appreciation of the music by listening intently to a recorded composition, (2) displaying appropriate body language, (3) avoiding doing other tasks while the music is playing, and (4) showing that you have prepared for the lesson by providing pertinent information on the composer, composition, and period. Students may *role-play* by presenting a pre-approved listening lesson to the class that reflects your listening example. With your help, other students may provide *performance feedback* by offering commendations or suggestions for improvement. *Transfer of training* occurs when students attend concerts or other events where they must display behavior that is appropriate for the situation and that reflects prior classroom instruction. These techniques are also effective for teaching various aspects of music and providing opportunities for students to take part in their learning.

With both Skill Streaming and Character Counts, the success of the behavior management approach depends on selecting the appropriate technique for the classroom situation and practicing positive behavior. In addition, the key to optimum success of any management plan is the involvement of the entire school in supporting the management system.

REFERENCES

Josephson Institute of Ethics. (2001). *Character Counts!* [On-line]. Available at: www.charactercounts.org.

Mann, J. H. (1956). Experimental evaluations of role-playing. *Psychological Bulletin, 53,* 227–34.

McGinnis, E., & Goldstein, A. (1984). *Skillstreaming the elementary school child.* Champaign, IL: Research Press Co.

Legal Issues in the Music Classroom

Because it requires individual as well as group effort, American public school music is a unique area of study. As in other core academic areas, music students are taught in groups and evaluated on individual achievement. However, performing ensembles are the major medium through which some general music and most upper secondary music instruction is given. The focus is still on the individual, but the individual also has responsibilities to the group, which is not common in other curricular subjects. Consequently, student achievement in music ensembles is realized both at the individual level and the group level through public concerts, usually outside of the regular school day. This unique arrangement results in a great deal of attention from school administrators and legal experts when considering discipline policies and how they are applied.

What Are the Legal Realities? Before any recommendation can be made about legal issues related to discipline, a few realities about the nature of courts and public schools are worthy of mention. First, because court judgments are constantly being made, legal interpretations are always in a state of flux. Consequently, educational law can be expected to change over time. Second, although the United States Supreme Court has addressed some school-related cases, most education policy is handled at the state level through legislation and judicial review. This results in some variation in discipline policies from state to state. Third, many school-related issues are open to interpretation or additional refinement at the local level. Thus, policies and procedures for discipline can vary by school district or even by school. Fourth, because of politics, tradition, or simple misunderstanding, policies and procedures in local schools may not necessarily follow the letter of the law. It often takes a lawsuit or threat of one to correct those practices. Fifth, because the news media give extensive coverage to court rulings, the courts can seem highly involved in influencing public school policy. In actuality, the courts generally shy away from most school-related issues. They recognize that school personnel are the experts at handling day-to-day operations and that some autonomy is needed to maintain order and discipline (McCarthy, Cambron-McCabe, & Thomas, 1998). Sixth, the courts, especially the federal courts, have only rarely addressed cases directly related to school music. Therefore, legal options for music teachers are usually inferred from other school-related cases. This can result in multiple interpretations.

All of this means that teachers must stay informed about legal issues in their state and local school districts through professional publications, in-service workshops, and informed administrators.

What Are the Issues? When looking at the big picture, legal issues related to discipline in music classrooms do not differ much from issues related to other academic and extracurricular areas. General school rules and procedures are the same, as are the administrative requirements for due process. However, several issues are of particular interest to music teachers, especially ensemble directors. These include the impact of student behavior on grades and ensemble membership, discipline policies during school trips, and the supervision and discipline of students by nonschool personnel.

When May Behavior Impact Grades and Ensemble Membership?

The beginning place for any grading or membership policy is to make sure it is consistent with the expectations and guidelines set forth by the state and local school district, that the school's administration is knowledgeable and supportive of it, and that details of the policy are announced at the beginning of the term so students know in advance what the course requirements are and what the consequences are for not fulfilling them. Failure to do this would violate the student's due process rights and could result in a grade or membership decision being overturned, regardless of how legal the criteria were (McCarthy, Cambron-McCabe, & Thomas, 1998).

One of the greatest concerns for ensemble directors is whether a student's grade can legally be lowered because of an unexcused absence during an after-school rehearsal or performance. For years, this type of grading arrangement was common at the secondary level. However, this practice has recently received greater scrutiny from some parents and administrators who see it as an unfair academic punishment. All the same, unless state laws specifically restrict such practices, courts have usually supported academic penalties for school absenteeism, assuming that such actions met due process requirements and were important to the educational process (McCarthy, Cambron-McCabe, & Thomas, 1998). For example, in a 1983 Missouri case (Johnson v. Shineman), a court of appeals upheld a grade that was reduced because a high school student missed band and chorus concerts without an acceptable excuse. As a result of the absences, the student received a failing grade for the second half-semester in band and chorus. The court noted that the student was informed about the performance requirements and penalty for not meeting them at the beginning of the semester.

Regarding ensemble membership, the courts have given great leeway to the local schools when determining who is eligible for participation and under what circumstances. This assumes that the criteria for membership are not unfairly discriminatory. A federal court decision in 1997 (Mazevski v. Horseheads Central School District) allowed the dismissal of a student from his high school's marching band, a graded class taken for academic credit, because he missed a performance for an unexcused reason. It was determined in this case that the student had no constitutionally protected right to membership. Although he was guaranteed a right to a public education, he was not automatically entitled to participate in each of its separate components. The court ruled that because he didn't comply with course requirements, he forfeited both his membership in the group and consequently his eligibility for all-state band. This ruling is particularly significant because it was handed down by the United States District Court for the Western District of New York. Although that court's judicial area is limited, the summary of this ruling drew from similar school-related cases across the country and could possibly be a reference for future decisions.

How Are Discipline Policies Impacted by School Trips? The courts have indicated that there is an increased responsibility for supervision when teachers take students off campus and into a less structured environment (McIntyre, 1990). Therefore, teachers are given greater authority for ensuring the safety and security of students. This can include sending students back home for breaking rules, although age-appropriate supervision is expected during the return trip.

The courts, as well as state and local policy makers, disagree on whether luggage may be inspected before leaving on a school trip. In one case, at least, it was suggested that parents be the ones to inspect their children's belongings before departing (McIntyre, 1990).

When May Nonschool Personnel Discipline Students? Another issue of concern for music educators is the role that nonschool personnel play in discipline policies. In most school music programs, a number of people typically have supervisory and instructional roles. Chaperones are the most common of these because of the many trips taken by school ensembles. Music directors also frequently hire nonschool personnel to teach private lessons or to help with color guard, percussion, or marching-band camp. Invariably, questions arise as to when and how these people may be involved in matters of discipline. School districts usually have some sort of established policy for the use of chaperones that logically should be followed. Still, it is important that the music teacher provide some sort of formal orientation for both chaperones and adjunct instructors. If no training is provided and one of these people administers a punishment out of line with school policy, then the supervising teacher could be held liable if a student sues.

REFERENCES

Johnson v. Shineman, 658 S.W. 2d 910 (Mo. Ct. App. 1983).

Mazevski v. Horseheads Central School District, 950 F. Supp. 69 (W.D.N.Y. 1997).

McCarthy, M., Cambron-McCabe, N., & Thomas, S. (1998). *Public school law: Teachers' and students' rights* (4th ed.). Boston: Allyn & Bacon.

McIntyre, R. A. (1990). Legal issues in the administration of public school music programs (Doctoral dissertation, University of Kansas). *Dissertation Abstracts International, 52,* 460.

Conclusion

Regardless of the type of management system implemented in the general, choral, and instrumental music classroom, some problems will persist. Even though these problems may be few, they can be frustrating and require disciplinary action beyond the teacher's expertise. It becomes necessary then for the teacher to create a response plan. In the elementary and middle school classroom, the plan may include a warning for the first offense, time-out for the second offense, a note or phone call home for the third offense, a conference with parents for the fourth offense, and a meeting in the principal's office for the fifth offense. At the high school level, a different procedure may be followed. Step 1 would be discussing the situation privately with the student. Step 2 would be to confer with the student's parent or guardian. Step 3 would be to refer the student to the principal.

Usually, most students will respond positively to the management systems discussed in this book. When management problems persist, it may mean that the teacher has not established a proper procedure for instruction. To establish a workable procedure, the teacher should (1) plan and organize the music curriculum, (2) devise effective instructional methodologies that include proper assessment of students' achievement and ability, and (3) anticipate, monitor, and correct student behavior. The successful music teacher will also anticipate most negative student behavior and plan the lesson with potential behavior problems in mind.

Music teachers must also be aware of the management image that they present and recognize the need to change their own behavior if their teaching style is ineffective. Taking a management profile assessment like the one in Chapter 1 could be very useful in determining whether a change is needed.

For optimum success in instituting any management plan, the entire school, school system, and community should support the plan. Two management systems that have been documented as being successful in kindergarten through twelfth grade are Character Counts and Skill Streaming. These systems address inappropriate behavior and teach students desirable qualities that help them become mature and responsible adults.

The music teacher must also prepare a plan for managing behavior in the music classroom that includes (1) knowing the students and the homes and communities from whence they come, (2) establishing guidelines, with student input, and (3) having the courage to discipline students if necessary. Using specific preventive measures will most likely reduce the need for disciplinary action. Whether in the general, choral, or instrumental music classroom, preventive steps should be well formulated. They may include (1) creating a supportive and positive environment, (2) utilizing up-to-date equipment that complements instruction, and (3) incorporating technology. In addition to preventive measures, the music teacher must develop sound strategies for addressing misbehavior while facilitating music learning. Some misbehavior requires minor intervention while other misbehavior demands more extreme actions. Whatever the requirement, discipline must be consistent and applied fairly. The Resources list at the back of this book provides sources for additional information.

Finally, music teachers should keep in mind that the decisions they make regarding classroom management may be scrutinized by administrators, parents, and legal experts. Therefore, they must stay informed about legal issues at the federal, state, and local levels that may impact their management plan. Teachers must also be capable of explaining and defending their policies on (1) how behavior affects grades and ensemble membership, (2) how discipline impacts school trips, and (3) when nonschool personnel, such as chaperones, may discipline students.

In the final analysis, music teachers must be adept in communicating the joy of music to students through carefully planned music instruction, varied musical experiences, and a well-thought-out and executed behavior management plan that maintains respect for all students and is defensible to administrators, parents, and the community.

Resources

Alexander, K., & Alexander, M. (1998). *American public school law* (4th ed.). Belmont, CA: Wadsworth Publishing Company.

ACE Presidents' Task Force on Teacher Education. (1999). *To touch the future: Transforming the way teachers are taught: An action agenda for college and university presidents.* Washington, DC: American Council on Education.

Antil, L., Jenkins, J., Wayne, S., & Vadasy, P. (1998). Cooperative learning: Prevalence, conceptualizations, and the relation between research and practice. *American Educational Research Journal, 35* (3), 419–54.

Brigham, F., Renfro, A., & Brigham, M. (1997). Linking music curriculum to teacher and student behavior. *Update: Applications of Research in Music Education, 15* (2), 24–28.

Brinson, B. A. (1996). *Choral music methods and materials.* New York: Schirmer Books.

Burton, L., & Takeo, K. (2000). *Soundplay: Understanding music through creative movement.* Reston, VA: MENC.

Cary, E., Levine, A., & Price, J. (1997). *The rights of students.* New York: Puffin Books.

Center for Adolescent Studies. (1996). What is your classroom management profile? *Teacher Talk, 1* (2) [On-line]. Available at http://www.education. indiana.edu/cas/

Cornett, C. E. (1999). *The arts as meaning makers.* Upper Saddle River, NJ: Prentice Hall.

Cruickshank, D. (1990). *Research that informs teachers and teacher educators.* Bloomington, IN: Phi Delta Kappa.

Doyle, W. (1986). Classroom organization and management. In M. C. Wittrock (Ed.), *Handbook of research on teaching* (3rd ed., pp. 392–431). New York: Macmillan.

Duke, R. (1999/2000). Measures of instructional effectiveness in music research. *Bulletin of the Council for Research in Music Education,* No. 143, 1–48.

Emmer, E. T., Evertson, C. M., & Worsham, M. E. (2000). *Classroom management for secondary teachers.* Boston: Allyn & Bacon.

Glaser, W. (1968). *Schools without failure.* New York: Harper & Row.

Good, T., & McCaslin, M. (1992). Teaching effectiveness. In M. C. Alkin (Ed.), *Encyclopedia of educational research, Vol. 4* (6th ed., pp. 1373–88). New York: Macmillan.

Gottfredson, D. (1992). Discipline. In M. C. Alkin (Ed.), *Encyclopedia of educational research, Vol. 1*(6th ed., pp. 331–34). New York: Macmillan.

Imber, M., & Van Geel, T. (2000). *Education law* (2nd ed.). Mahwah, NJ: Lawrence Erlbaum Associates.

Johnson, D., Johnson, R., & Stanne, M. B. (2000). *Cooperative learning methods: A meta-analysis* [On-line]. Minneapolis, MN: University of Minnesota. Available at http://www.clcrc.com/pages/cl-methods.html.

Johnson v. Shineman, 658 S.W. 2d 910 (Mo. Ct. App. 1983).

Josephson Institute of Ethics. (2001). *Character Counts!* [On-line]. Available at: www.charactercounts.org.

Kaplan, P., & Stauffer, S. (1994). *Cooperative learning in music.* Reston, VA: MENC.

Kowalski, K. (2000). *Teen rights: At home, at school, online.* Berkeley Heights, NJ: Enslow Publishers.

Lemlech, J. K. (1979). *Classroom management.* New York: Harper & Row.

Levin, J., & Nolan, J. F. (1991). *Principles of classroom management: A hierarchical approach.* Englewood Cliffs, NJ: Prentice Hall.

Madsen, C., Standley, J., & Cassidy, J. (1989). Demonstration and recognition of high and low contrasts in teacher intensity. *Journal of Research in Music Education, 37* (2), 85–92.

Mann, J. H. (1956). Experimental evaluations of role-playing. *Psychological Bulletin, 53,* 227–34.

Mazevski v. Horseheads Central School District, 950 F. Supp.69 (W.D.N.Y. 1997).

McCarthy, M., Cambron-McCabe, N., & Thomas, S. (1998). *Public school law: Teachers' and students' rights* (4th ed.). Boston: Allyn & Bacon.

McGinnis, E., & Goldstein, A. P. (1984). *Skillstreaming the elementary school child.* Champaign, IL: Research Press Company.

McIntyre, R. A. (1990). Legal issues in the administration of public school music programs (Doctoral dissertation, University of Kansas, 1990). *Dissertation Abstracts International, 52,* 460.

Merriam-Webster's collegiate dictionary (10th ed.). (1998). Springfield, MA: Merriam-Webster.

Rossman, L. R. (1989). *TIPS: Discipline in the music classroom.* Reston, VA: MENC.

Royse, D. (1989). Significant predictors of concert band membership continuation or discontinuation by nonmusic major students at three selected universities (Doctoral dissertation, Kent State University, 1989). *Dissertation Abstracts International, 50,* 2823.

Saunders, T. C., & Worthington, J. L. (1990). Teacher effectiveness in the performance classroom. *Update: Applications of Research in Music Education, 8* (2), 26–29.

Short, P. M., Short, R. J., & Blanton, C. (1994). *Rethinking student discipline: Alternatives that work.* Thousand Oaks, CA: Corwin Press.

Swears, L. (1984). *Teaching the elementary school chorus.* West Nyack, NY: Parker.

Acknowledgments

The authors would like to express their appreciation to Robert Shoop, professor of educational law at Kansas State University, for his input on legal issues. Special thanks are extended to Pamela Jackson, Deborah Roberts, Elizabeth Welch, Christine Bock, and Amanda Ragan, Knox (TN) County music teachers, for sharing their expertise in managing student behavior at the elementary level. Finally, we thank Teresa Hodges for her clerical assistance in preparing the materials to be published.